D1097366

Coop. Minerva Editrice
ASSISI

LAUDES CREATURARUM

ST. FRANCIS OF ASSISI

Drawings by
ELISABETH HOLLEY

Most high, omnipotent, great Lord,
to You all praise, glory and honor
and every blessing
To You alone, Most high, do they belong
and no man is worthy to pronounce
Your name
Praise be to You my Lord
with all Your creatures
Especially Messer Brother Sun
Who illuminates the day for us
And he is beautiful and radiant
with great splendor
And from You, Most high, brings meaning.
Praise be to You my Lord
for Sister Moon and for the stars
In Heaven You have formed them,
Shining and precious and fair.
Praise be to You my Lord
for Brother Wind
For air and clouds, clear sky
and every sort of weather
by which means You sustain
Your creatures.
Praise be to You my Lord
For Sister Water
She is useful

And humble, precious and pure.
Praise be to You my Lord
For Brother Fire
Through him You enlighten the night
And he is fair and merry
And vital and strong.
Praise be to You my Lord
For our sister Mother Earth
Who nourishes and sustains us all
and brings forth divers fruits
with many–colored flowers and herbs.
Praise be to You my Lord
For those who pardon grant
For love of You
And who bear infirmity and tribulation.
Blessed be those who live in peace
For by You, Most high,
will they be crowned.
Praise be to You my Lord
For our Sister Bodily Death
From whom no living man can flee,
Woe to those who die in mortal sin;
Blessed be those who are found
in Your holy Will
For the second death will not harm them
Praise and bless my Lord and thank Him
and serve Him with great humility.

Most high, omnipotent, great Lord,
to You all praise, glory and honor
and every blessing
To You alone, Most high,
do they belong
and no man is worthy to pronounce
Your name

Praise be to You my Lord
with all Your creatures

Especially Messer Brother Sun
Who illuminates the day for us
And he is beautiful and radiant
with great splendor
And from You, Most high,
brings meaning.

Praise be to You my Lord
for Sister Moon and for the stars
In Heaven You have formed them,
Shining and precious and fair.

Praise be to You my Lord
for Brother Wind
For air and clouds, clear sky
and every sort of weather
by which means You sustain
Your creatures.

Praise be to You my Lord
For Sister Water
She is useful
And humble, precious and pure.

Praise be to You my Lord
For Brother Fire
Through him You enlighten the night
And he is fair and merry
And vital and strong.

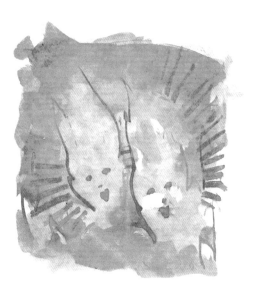

Praise be to You my Lord
For our sister Mother Earth
Who nourishes and sustains us all
and brings forth divers fruits
with many–colored flowers
and herbs.

Praise be to You my Lord
For those who pardon grant
For love of You
And who bear infirmity
and tribulation.
Blessed be those who live in peace
For by You, Most high,
will they be crowned.

Praise be to You my Lord
For our Sister Bodily Death
From whom no living man can flee,
Woe to those who die in mortal sin;

Blessed be those who are found
in Your holy Will
For the second death
will not harm them
Praise and bless my Lord
and thank Him
and serve Him with great humility.

Printed
by Arti Grafiche Antica Porziuncola
Cannara (Pg)